Baby Quilts

Baby Quilts

15 Original Designs for Every Nursery Décor

EDITED BY LINDA NEUBAUER

Creative Publishing international

CHANHASSEN, MN

Creative Publishing international

Copyright 2006

Creative Publishing international
18705 Lake Drive East
Chanhassen, Minnesota 55317
1-800-328-3895
www.creativepub.com
All rights reserved

President/CEO: Ken Fund
Vice President/Publisher: Linda Ball
Vice President/Retail Sales: Kevin Haas

Executive Editor: Alison Brown Cerier
Senior Editor: Linda Neubauer
Photo Stylist: Joanne Wawra
Creative Director: Brad Springer
Photo Art Director: Tim Himsel
Photographer: Steve Galvin
Production Manager: Laura Hokkanen

Cover Design: Michaelis Carpelis Design
Page Design and Layout: Brian Donahue / bedesign, inc.

Acknowledgments
The following companies supplied products for the projects indicated:
The Warm Company (pages 83, 89, and 93), Sulky of America (page 83), Wimpole Street
Creations (page 83), Janome America, Inc. (page 83), Benartex (pages 9, 15, and 19).

Library of Congress Cataloging-in-Publication Data
Baby quilts : 15 original designs for every nursery décor / edited by Linda Neubauer.
    p. cm.
  ISBN 1-58923-251-8 (soft cover)
  1. Quilting--Patterns. 2. Patchwork--Patterns. 3. Children's quilts. I. Neubauer, Linda.
  TT835.B215 2006
  746.46'041--dc22

                        2005026488

Printed in China
10 9 8 7 6 5 4 3 2 1

Contents

Sewing Baby Quilts

What more thoughtful gift could you make for a newborn than a cuddly baby quilt? With loving attention to every stitch, a quilt shares your creative talent, provides warmth and comfort, and becomes a treasured keepsake for the child.

We wanted the projects in this book to represent a variety of styles and quilting techniques, so we asked for projects from five talented designers and gave each of them different guidelines. Gerri Robinson designed three quilts that feature very textured fabrics and unexpected surface effects. Susan Stein's quilts are block-pieced in unique ways with vibrant, contemporary colors. Sharon Hultgren developed three foundation-pieced quilt patterns, each with a very distinctive look. Janis Bullis provided us with three cuddly appliquéd baby quilts. Phyllis Dobbs designed quick-and-easy quilts with large center panels, big blocks, and wide borders. There is sure to be a project to suit every quilter and every baby.

Each project has a complete materials list, cutting instructions, and step-by-step directions for sewing the quilt tops. How you quilt and bind the quilts is usually a matter of personal preference, though special instructions are provided for some of the projects. The materials lists include the fabrics and notions you need to buy but don't include the things you probably have on hand, such as measuring and cutting tools, marking pens, quilter's safety pins, and sewing thread. All seam allowances are ¼" (6 mm) wide and are included in the cutting directions and templates.

You can copy the designs closely or choose different fabrics and colors to suit the nursery décor or the preferences of the parents. With the fifteen designs in this book and a world of quilting fabrics to choose from, the possibilities for baby quilts are unlimited. Pick your favorite and let the quilting begin!

Super Plush

Minkee block quilt

$\mathcal{I}$f you have never touched the wonderful Minkee fabrics by Benartex, you are in for a real treat. They are so plush and soothing, you can't stop yourself from "petting" them. Just imagine how gentle and comforting they would be in a baby quilt!

Minkee fabrics are now widely available in quilt shops and other fabric stores, and people are looking for new ways to use them. To make the most of the texture, this quilt is made up of simple blocks. I chose bright colors and Dalmatian spots. You can opt for the pastel colors, if you prefer. Because of the natural thickness and body of Minkee fabrics, batting isn't necessary in this quilt.

Gerri Robinson

FINISHED SIZE: 48" × 58" (122 × 147 cm)

TECHNIQUES USED: Quilting with textured fabric, mitered-corner binding

Cutting Directions

One 6½" (16.3 cm) full crosswise strip of each Blankee color; cut seven 6½" (16.3 cm) squares from each strip

Three 6½" (16.3 cm) full crosswise strips of Dalmatian; cut 14 6½" (16.3 cm) squares from two strips; cut seven 3½" × 6½" (9 × 16.3 cm) rectangles from the third strip

Four 3½" (9 cm) full crosswise strips of Dalmatian for borders

Four 3½" (9 cm) full crosswise strips of binding fabric

Materials

- ¼ yd. (0.25 m) each of six colors of Benartex Minkee Blankee fabric: purple, orange, yellow, fuchsia, royal blue, green
- 1 yd. (0.92 m) Dalmatian Minkee Skin
- 1⅞ yd. (1.75 m) Minkee fabric of choice for backing
- ½ yd. (0.5 m) Minkee fabric of choice for binding

Designer's Tip

To sew on Minkee fabrics, use a universal needle, size 80/12. Attach a walking foot to your machine to help the layers feed evenly. If pressing is necessary, set the iron on medium setting and press lightly to avoid stretching the fabric.

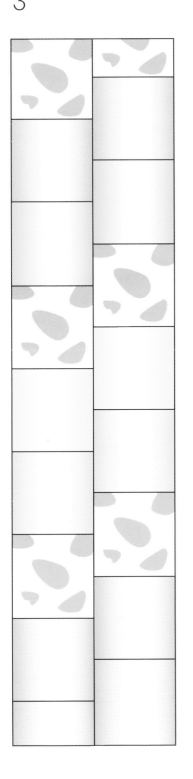

3

1. Arrange the pieces in order on a design wall or work surface, using the photograph on page 8 as a guide.

2. Stitch the pieces of each column together. Lightly press the seam allowances open.

3. Stitch the columns together, matching the seams in one column to the centers of the squares in the next column.

4. Measure the quilt top to bottom through the center. Cut two border strips to this length. Sew the borders to the sides of the quilt. Press the seam allowances toward the borders.

5. Measure the quilt side to side through the center, including the side borders. Cut two border strips to this length. Sew the borders to the top and bottom of the quilt. Press the seam allowances toward the borders.

6. Cut the backing to the same size as the quilt top. Place the backing and quilt top wrong sides together. Machine-baste ¼" (6 mm) from the outer edges. Baste the layers together with safety pins placed about 6" (15 cm) apart.

7. Quilt by machine. The quilt on page 8 was quilted free-motion in alternating rows of circles and lines. Following the diagram, you can stitch from one side of the quilt to the other without stopping.

8. Join the binding strips with diagonal seams; press the seams open. Bind the quilt, using the continuous method and mitering the corners as on page 28, steps 16 to 18. Stitch ½" (1.3 cm) from the edge instead of the usual ⅜" (1 cm) to allow for the extra bulk of the fabric.

7

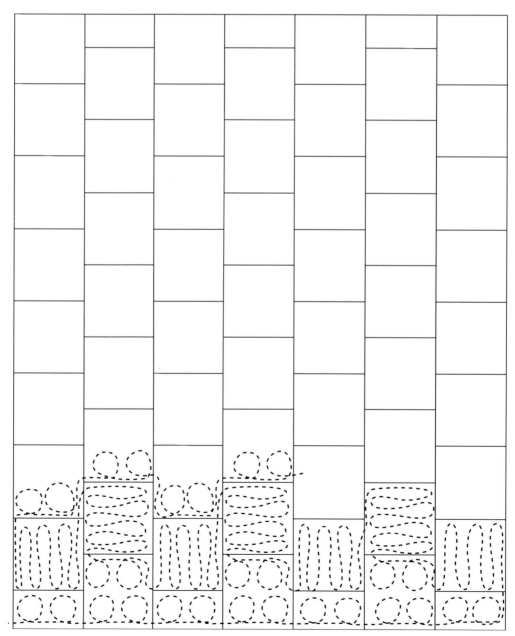

8

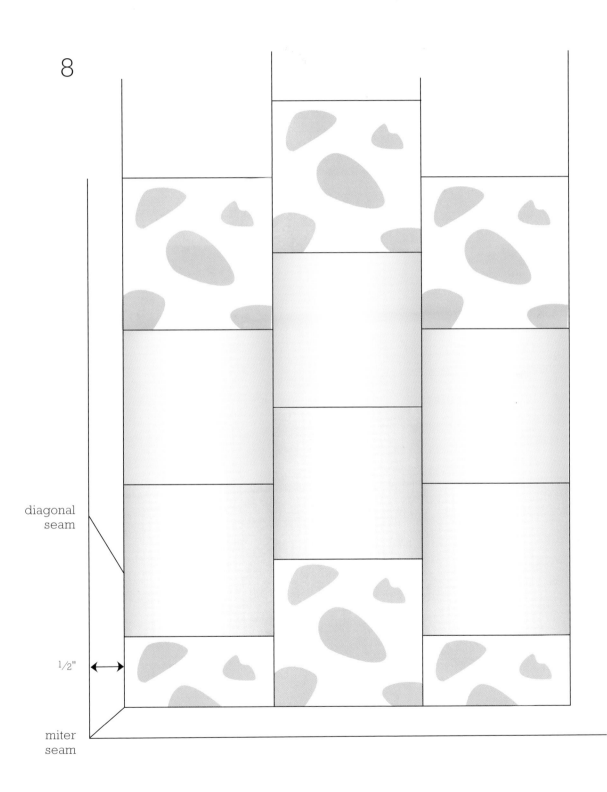

diagonal
seam

1/2"

miter
seam

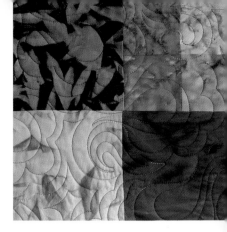

Soft Touch

Flannel block quilt

Flannel fabrics, with their softness and warmth, make cuddly quilts for babies. For this bold block quilt, I used a collection of brightly colored flannels that have a printed background for visual texture, too. Large blocks and four-patch blocks are arranged randomly throughout the quilt to create an interesting collage of color. Choose a variety of light and medium values in both warm and cool colors to achieve this look.

Gerri Robinson

Finished Size: 46" × 52" (117 × 132 cm)

Techniques Used: Simple block piecing

Cutting Directions

Twenty-eight 6½" (16.3 cm) squares of brightly colored flannels

Three 3½" (9 cm) crosswise strips each of the warm and cool colors for the four-patch blocks

One 5" (12.7 cm) full crosswise strip of each fabric for top and bottom borders

Two 5" (12.7 cm) full crosswise strips of each fabric for side borders

Materials

- One fat quarter each of eight different flannel fabrics for large blocks
- One fat quarter each of four different brightly colored flannels for four-patch blocks (two warm and two cool colors)
- ¼ yd. (0.25 m) each of two flannels for top and bottom borders
- ⅓ yd. (0.32 m) each of two flannels for side borders
- ½ yd. (0.5 m) flannel for binding
- 3 yd. (2.75 m) flannel for backing
- One low-loft crib batting

1. Sew a cool strip to a warm strip lengthwise, joining three sets of the same color combination. Press the seam allowances toward the cool strips. Cut the strips into 14 units 3½" (9 cm) wide. These will be called unit 1.

2. Sew the other cool strips to the other warm strips lengthwise, joining three sets of the same color combination. Press the seam allowances toward the cool strips. Cut the strips into 14 units 3½" (9 cm) wide. These will be called unit 2.

1

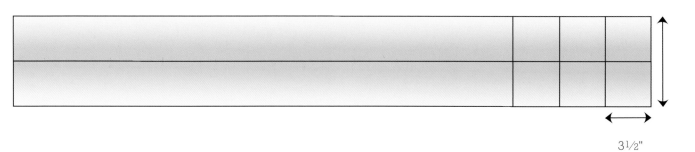

6½"

3½"

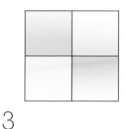

3

3. Sew each unit 1 to a unit 2 to create 14 four-patch blocks. Press the seam allowances toward 2.

4. Arrange the four-patch blocks and the 6½" (16.3 cm) blocks on a design wall or work surface, following the photograph on page 14. Sew the blocks together in rows.

5. Sew the rows together, aligning seams.

6. Measure the quilt side to side through the center. Cut border strips to this length. Sew one to the top and one to the bottom of the quilt. Press the seam allowances toward the borders.

7. Measure the quilt top to bottom through the center, including the top and bottom borders. Piece two border strips together, press the seam allowances open, and cut the border to this length. Repeat for the other side border. Sew one border to each side of the quilt. Press the seam allowances toward the borders.

8. Press the quilt top. Piece the backing. Cut the backing and batting slightly larger than the quilt top. Layer the backing, batting, and quilt top; baste with safety pins or by hand.

9. Quilt as desired. If you prefer to see your thread on your quilt, use a heavier quilting thread. The lighter threads will sink down into the flannel fibers.

10. Bind the quilt as desired.

Designer's Tip

I do not prewash or preshrink any of my fabric. When the quilt is completely finished, I toss it in a gentle wash and a tumble dry cycle so all the fabrics and batting will shrink together. I love the soft, rumpled look. I do use a fabric dye sheet, such as Shout Color Catcher, in the wash cycle to catch any excess color that may bleed. This has always worked for me and no quilt has ever been ruined.

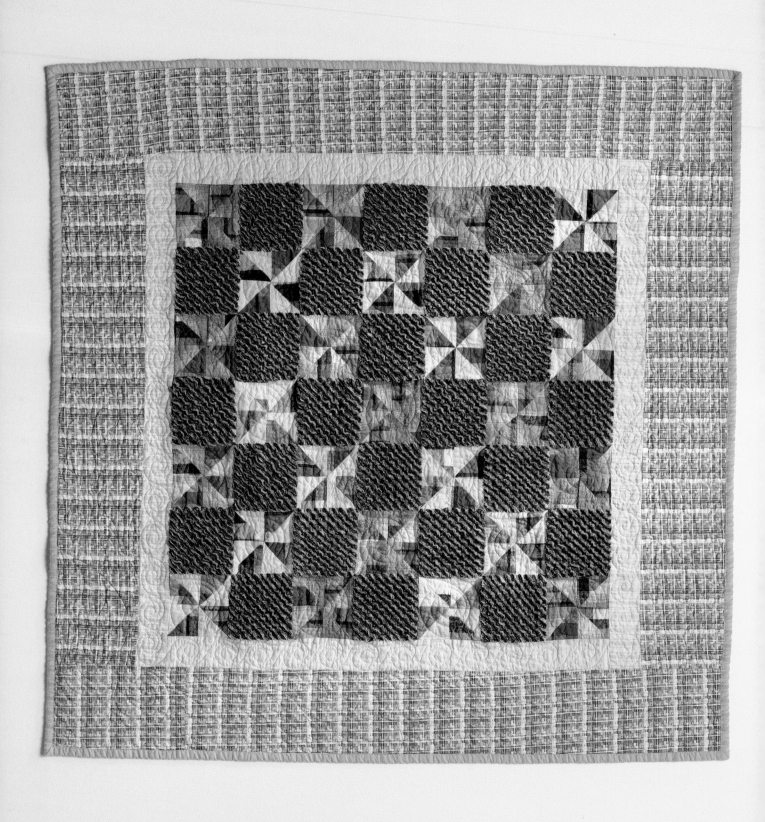

Warm Fuzzies

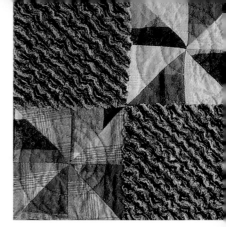

Chenille and pinwheels quilt

his quilt is fun to look at and just as much fun to touch! Babies love to explore with their fingers new textures like the rumpled ridges of the faux chenille squares in this quilt. Layers of fabrics are sewn together in bias channels and then the top layers are slashed. When the quilt is washed the first time, the slashed edges fluff up to create the look of chenille.

Experiment with the fabrics for your chenille squares. Fabrics that have color on both sides work the best, and you'll need five layers. Sometimes just changing the order of the fabrics makes a big difference.

Gerri Robinson

Finished Size: 44" × 44" (112 × 112 cm)

Techniques Used: Faux chenille, pinwheel blocks

Materials

- ¼ yd. (0.25 m) each of five fabrics for pinwheels: pink, yellow, lime green, turquoise, and multi
- 1 yd. (0.92 m) each of five fabrics for chenille squares: multi, yellow, turquoise/black, pink, green/turquoise
- ⅓ yd. (0.32 m) yellow fabric for inner border
- ¾ yd. (0.7 m) plaid fabric for outer border
- 1⅜ yd. (1.3 m) fabric, 45" (115 cm) wide or 2¾ yd. (2.55 m) if narrower, for backing
- One low-loft crib batting
- ⅜ yd. (0.35 m) lime green fabric for binding
- Clover Slash Cutter or sharp embroidery scissors

Cutting Directions

One 2⅞" (7.2 cm) full crosswise strip of pink; cut into 14 squares, each cut in half diagonally to yield 28 triangles for pinwheels

One 2⅞" (7.2 cm) full crosswise strip of yellow, lime green, and turquoise; cut 12 squares from each strip then cut each in half diagonally to yield 24 triangles of each color for pinwheels

Four 2⅞" (7.2 cm) full crosswise strips of multicolor fabric; cut into 50 squares; then cut each in half diagonally to yield 100 triangles for pinwheels

Three 15" (38 cm) squares from each of the five fabrics for chenille blocks

Four 2½" (6.5 cm) full crosswise strips of fabric for inner border

Four 6" (15 cm) full crosswise strips of fabric for outer border

Four 2½" (6.5 cm) full crosswise strips of binding fabric

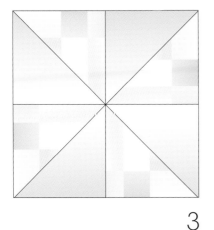

3

5

1. Place a multicolor triangle and a solid color triangle right sides together. Stitch together on the long, bias edge, taking care not to stretch the seam.

2. Press the seam allowances toward the multicolored fabric. Trim off the "dog ears."

3. Repeat steps 1 and 2 for all the triangles to make 100 triangle squares. Sew them together in matching sets of four to make 25 pinwheel blocks with a finished size of 4½" (11.5 cm) square.

4. Layer the 15" (38 cm) squares of fabric, right sides up, in order from bottom to top: multicolor, yellow, turquoise/black, pink, green/turquoise. You will have three sets of five fabrics each. Pin the layers together, inserting the pins in diagonal rows.

5. Sew the layers together in a diagonal line from corner to corner. Reverse the direction and sew another line ⅝" (1.5 cm) from the first one. Continue sewing lines ⅝" (1.5 cm) apart, reversing the direction, until you reach the outer corner. Then sew lines on the opposite side of the center. Repeat for each set of layered squares.

Designer's Tip

A Clover Slash Cutter is designed specifically for making faux chenille. It has a narrow guide that slides into the channel just above the foundation layer and a small rotary cutter that slashes the upper layers. Small, sharp embroidery scissors also work well for slashing the fabrics. Take care not to cut the bottom layer.

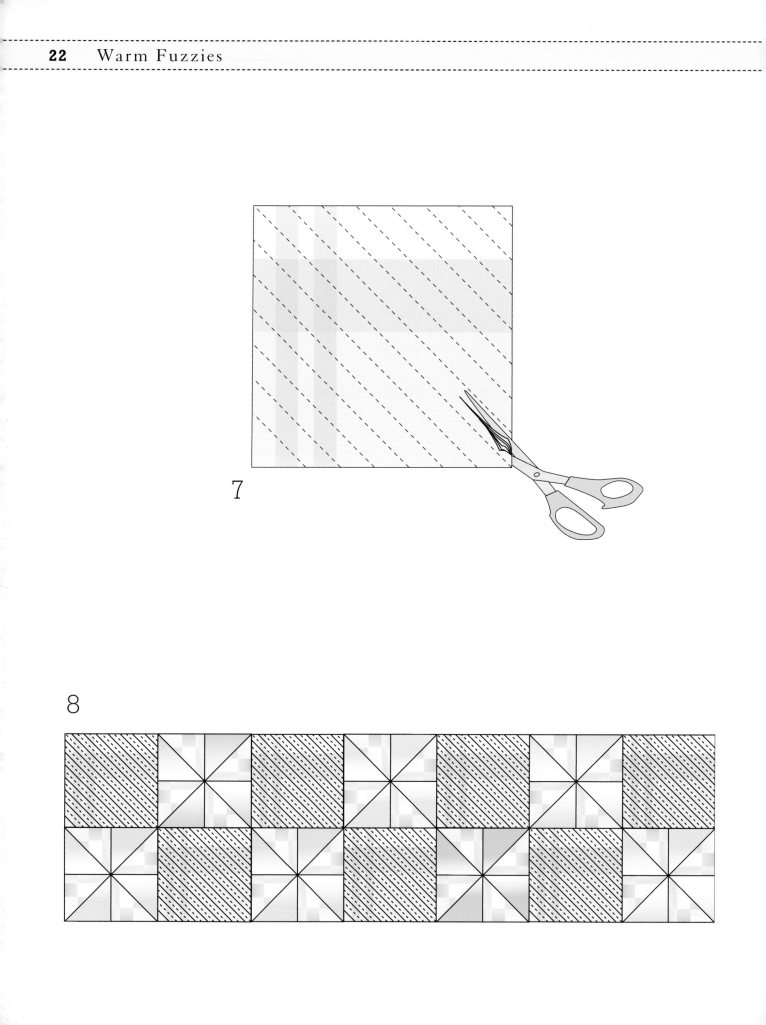

7

8